Contents

Look for the Then and Now boxes. They highlight parts of Aztec culture that are present in our modern world.

Any words appearing in the text in bold, **like this**, are explained in the glossary.

What did the Aztecs do for me?

Aztec warriors were fierce. They marched into battle carrying shields made of wooden canes woven with heavy cotton and decorated with brightly coloured feathers. They fought with bows and arrows, spears, slings, clubs, and saw-like weapons. These saw-swords were made of wood edged with strips of sharp glass called obsidian. Musicians played pipes, drums, and trumpets made from large shells while the men fought.

Aztecs usually did not try to kill their enemies. Instead, Aztec warriors wanted to take as many prisoners as possible. The more prisoners a warrior took, the more decorated he became. Successful warriors wore colourful cloaks and feathers, and painted their faces red and yellow. The *tlatoani*, or emperor, rewarded his best warriors with food, clothing, and land.

Do we really have anything in common with this warlike people? Look at the picture below. It seems very different to modern times, but you might be surprised to discover some things the Aztecs did that we still do today.

Who were the Aztecs?

Five hundred years ago, the Aztecs controlled a large area of land in what is now central Mexico. Before they moved there in about 1150, they probably lived in northern Mexico or the south-western United States. Different groups travelled down to central Mexico at different times. They established villages and towns throughout the mountainous region.

This map shows the Aztec Empire around 1500, when it was at its biggest and most powerful.

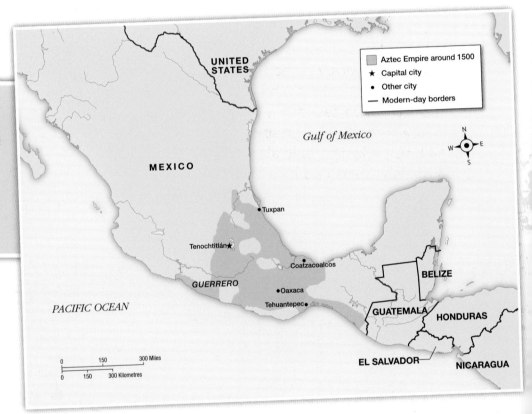

A warrior people

By 1520, about 300,000 Aztecs lived in the city of Tenochtitlán. Up to two million people lived in nearby valleys and plains. Each city had its own *tlatoani*, who kept an army to defend his people against attack and to **conquer** others.

The Aztecs went to war to gain more wealth and to expand their **empire**, not to destroy other cities. Defeated neighbours had to pay **tributes** to the winning *tlatoani*. Tributes were paid in gold, feathered headdresses, shields, woven cloth, precious stones, and chillies. The *tlatoani* could use these himself or have them sold for him in the marketplace.

Conquerors from Spain

Tenochtitlán was the capital of the Aztec Empire and Moctezuma II was its *tlatoani*. When the Spanish **conquistador** Hernán Cortés arrived in Aztec lands in 1519, Moctezuma sent him gifts. Moctezuma hoped Cortés and his men would return to Spain. Instead, the beautiful gold, jewellery, and cloth showed Cortés that the Aztecs were rich. He wanted their wealth for Spain. Despite its great power and wealth, the Aztec Empire lasted only about 100 years (1427–1521) before the Spanish destroyed it.

A strange test

The Aztecs had never seen people like the Spanish before. To find out whether they were gods or men, the Aztecs sent the Spanish food and slaves. If they were gods, they would kill the slaves and drink their blood. The Spanish proved themselves to be only humans by eating the food and letting the slaves live!

This 1579 painting shows Hernán Cortés being presented with a gift sent by Moctezuma.

What was Aztec society like?

Aztec society was divided into two main groups: commoners and nobles. There were also warriors, who came from both groups.

Nobles and commoners

The nobles were the richest 5–10 per cent of the population. They elected the *tlatoani* and lived on the **tributes** paid by commoners and **conquered** peoples.

Most common people were farmers. Some were builders or artists and craftsmen. They usually lived together according to their job. For example, craftsmen and their families lived in one area and builders and their families in another. The leader of each neighbourhood group was a noble who collected tributes.

This illustration shows how a wealthy Aztec noble would have dressed.

THEN...

The people of central Mexico spoke the **Nahuatl** language. Nahuatl is related to the languages spoken by the Comanche, Pima, Shoshone, and other tribes of western North America. Since all the people in central Mexico spoke Nahuatl, communication between different cities was not difficult.

Warriors

All Aztec boys were trained to become warriors. Most of them did this for only part of their time, while also working as farmers, fishermen, or in other trades. The most talented boys could become professional soldiers, which was considered a very good job. The *tlatoani* needed these skilled warriors to lead his army into battle.

Hair

Aztec boys had shaved heads. At the age of 10, boys were allowed to start growing a tuft of hair on the back of their head. A boy could not cut the hair until he had captured an enemy. If he still had his hair after three battles, people called him a coward.

These Mexicans are celebrating their history. They are among the one million Mexicans who still speak Nahuatl.

...NOW

Some English words that we use today come from Nahuatl. They include: tomato (*tomatl*), avocado (*ahuacatl*), chocolate (*chocolatl*), and coyote (*coyotl*).

Marriage and family

Family life was important to the Aztecs. When a boy reached his late teens or early twenties, his parents would arrange a marriage for him. Girls were usually married at about the age of 15.

Aztec women ran their homes, looked after their children, and wove and embroidered cloth. They also worked as healers and traders. An Aztec woman could own property and make her own decisions.

Here, an Aztec woman is cooking outside her family home. Small groups of houses were surrounded by an **adobe** wall.

THEN...

In Aztec times, some work belonged to men, while other work was women's work. The beautiful red capes worn by nobles and warriors required the skills of both men and women. The red dye came from crushed **cochineal insects** that fed off the prickly pear cactus. Farmers brushed the insects from cactus, dried them, cleaned them, and crushed them to make dye. Women wove the cloth and dyed it red. This brilliant red colour was also used as paint.

Children

Aztec parents loved their children, but they were very strict with them. Mothers looked after all the smallest children, but when boys were three years old, their fathers would take charge of them. Boys would help their fathers carry loads to the marketplace. Girls stayed at home with their mothers and learned how to run a household and weave cloth.

Stretching ceremony

Every 260 days, the Aztecs held a special stretching ceremony. Parents pulled on their children's noses, necks, ears, fingers, and legs to help them grow properly!

These cactus leaves, hanging in a shed, are covered with white clusters of cochineal insects.

...NOW

Today, cochineal insects from Mexico are still used as red food colouring around the world. Beginning in 2011, products sold in the United States that use insect dye will have the words cochineal extract or **carmine** on the ingredient label. It takes about 140 thousand insects to make 1 kilogram (2 pounds) of colouring used in food.

How did the Aztecs worship?

Most Aztec priests came from the noble class. They began their training at about six years of age. They learned all about the gods and goddesses and how to care for **shrines**. Priests were very powerful in Aztec society.

Human sacrifice

Aztecs believed that a god called Quezalcoatl made people with blood from his own body. In return, people had to feed the gods with offerings of blood, especially the blood from a human heart. Captured enemy warriors and slaves were killed as **human sacrifices**.

This painting from 1579 shows Aztec priests removing the heart of their victim during a human sacrifice.

THEN...

The Aztecs believed that when a person died, their soul went to Mictlan, the Land of the Dead. Their family wrapped the body in cloth, burned it, and buried the ashes under the floor of their house. Every August, a festival was held to honour the goddess of the dead, Mictecacihuatl. People thought that the dead came back to join in the fun.

The sacrifices were held on festival days. They were carried out by priests, on the tops of **pyramid** temples. Crowds of people gathered to watch. The Aztecs believed that sacrifices brought good luck and good harvests.

This modern Mexican woman is celebrating the Day of the Dead by dressing up and painting her face to look like a skull.

Death of a warrior

When a warrior was killed in battle, the Aztecs thought that his soul would go to the heaven of the Sun, where it would become a butterfly or hummingbird and could fly back to Earth.

...NOW

Mexicans today continue to honour the dead at a festival called the Day of the Dead on 2 November. Families build small shrines in their homes in memory of their dead relatives. Friends and neighbours come to pray at the shrines and everybody visits the cemetery. There is lots of food and music, and people tell stories about when their relatives were alive.

Healing the sick

Aztec priests were also healers. They used medicines made from plants to treat illnesses, and prayed for people to get well again. Women were often healers, too. They helped other women in childbirth and knew a lot about diseases.

Battlefield medicine

On the battlefield, healers cleaned wounds, applied medicines, and used clean cloths as bandages. Medicines made from the maguey plant and prickly pear cactus were used to stop infections and to treat broken bones. These treatments worked very well. The Spanish **conquistadors** noticed that Aztec warriors did not die from the same kinds of wounds that often killed their own soldiers.

Bathing

At a time when Europeans never bathed, the Aztecs used to take regular baths. Aztec mothers taught their children to wash their hands.

THEN...

Soon after the Spanish defeated the Aztecs, they wrote about Aztec medicines. These accounts, which included drawings of medicinal plants, were sent back to Spain. They included cures for heart pain, lung diseases, bad breath, armpit odour, and stomach rumbling.

Prickly pear leaves are still used in Mexico. Here, they are being sold at a local market.

...NOW

Today doctors use many of the healing plants first discovered by the Aztecs. The prickly pear cactus was not only eaten by the Aztecs but also used as medicine. In 2007, a medical study proved that the prickly pear cactus is useful in treating **diabetes**. It can also be used to heal burns and stop bleeding. Scientists continue to study the plants used by Aztec healers in the hope of rediscovering Aztec cures.

What games did the Aztecs play?

Patolli

Both nobles and commoners enjoyed a game called patolli. Each player tossed beans on to a cross-shaped board. The first player to return the beans to their starting point won the game. Prizes were valuable items such as jewellery, cloaks, and the feathers of the brightly coloured quetzal bird.

This Aztec drawing from the 1500s shows nobles playing a game of patolli.

THEN...

Ullamaliztli players used a solid rubber ball that bounced. This amazed the Spanish **conquistadors**. They had never seen anything made of rubber before. The Aztecs also used rubber for dolls, sandals, medicine, and lip balm. They even had rubber bands, which they used to attach stone axe heads to wooden handles.

Ullamaliztli

Another favourite game was ullamaliztli, which was usually just for nobles. Crowds of people would watch as two teams played each other on an L-shaped court with walls. Players used their hips or knees to hit a ball. There were many ways of scoring points, but the hardest was to hit the ball through a stone ring in the wall.

This illustration shows Aztec men playing ullamaliztli. Do you think you would be able to hit the ball through the ring?

Chewing gum

The Aztecs used a sticky gum from the *Manilkara chicle* tree, called chicle, to make chewing gum. They used it to keep their breath fresh, but chewing gum in front of others was bad manners!

...NOW

In 1839, the American Charles Goodyear made a new kind of rubber that soon became used all over the world. However, the Aztecs invented rubber first. It took until 1999 for archaeologists to learn how the Aztecs did it. They mixed fluid from the *Castilla elastica* tree with the juice of the morning glory vine. Then, using their hands, they formed the mixture into the shapes they needed.

What did the Aztecs eat?

The Aztecs grew and made many different kinds of food. They ate maize (corn) in soups and stews. They made tortillas (flat bread), and tamales (meat packed in dough). They also ate lots of beans, peppers, squash, tomatoes, and avocadoes.

Aztecs farmed the land, went fishing, and hunted animals for food.

Sources of protein

The nearby lakes provided the Aztecs with all kinds of food, such as fish, lake shrimp, and frogs. Aztecs even liked to eat salamanders, water bugs, and lake worms!

Farmers and hunters sold lots of animals for their meat at the market. The Aztecs ate turkeys, hairless dogs, deer, rabbits, mice, armadillos, snakes, and iguanas.

THEN...

Salvia hispanica is a kind of grain that the Aztecs called chia. They believed that eating it gave their warriors energy.

Tecuicatl

Tecuicatl is a slimy green plant that grows in Lake Texcoco, central Mexico. Aztec farmers collected the plant, dried it, and made it into loaves. The loaves were cut up into small pieces for eating. Tecuicatl lasted for up to a year. It was full of vitamins that kept people healthy.

Chocolate

Chocolate was too expensive for most people to eat or drink. Soldiers were allowed to eat it, and it was sometimes given to them in their rations. The *tlatoani* could afford to drink it himself and serve it to his guests. It was often flavoured with peppers, cornmeal, and spices.

Adding the ground seeds of the chia plant to food and drink may help prevent some diseases.

Popcorn

The Aztecs liked to eat popcorn. When the Spanish tried it, they liked it enough to take it back to Spain. The Spanish **conquistador** Hernán Cortés wrote that the corn "makes itself look like a very white flower".

...NOW

They were right! Scientists say that chia is very good for us. It may also help prevent heart disease and **diabetes**.

Traders

Tenochtitlán's traders travelled far to exchange rabbit fur, cloth, and jewellery for feathers, seashells, and precious stones such as jade and turquoise. Craftsmen needed these items to make clothing and ornaments for the nobles. Traders sold their goods in the Aztec market.

Sometimes, traders would also worked as spies. When they brought useful information from other cities, towns, and villages to the Aztecs, the *tlatoani* would reward them.

Crowds

It is thought that around 25,000 people visited the market in Tenochtitlán every day. On special occasions, as many as 50,000 people may have shopped there!

Money

The Aztecs used cloth or **cacao beans** as money. Twenty large, white, cotton cloaks could buy enough food to feed a family for a year. Cacao beans were used to buy smaller items. A Spanish account written in 1545 suggests that:

- A bundle of firewood = 1 cacao bean
- 1 tomato = 1 cacao bean
- 1 avocado = 3 cacao beans
- 1 rabbit = 30 cacao beans

THEN...

The Spanish **conquistador** Hernán Cortés saw tomatoes growing in Moctezuma II's gardens. He took some seeds back to Spain with him. People all over Europe began to plant tomatoes in their gardens because of their bright colour. However, they didn't eat them. They thought they were poisonous.

This mural, painted by Mexican artist Diego Rivera, shows traders and shoppers at the great Aztec market at Tlateloco, near Tenochtitlán.

...NOW

People all over the world eat and enjoy tomatoes, cooked and uncooked, in sauces, salads, on pizza, and served in many other ways. It was probably the Italians who first ate them in Europe, and many Italian dishes now use tomato sauce. Tomatoes are very good for us.

Why was Tenochtitlán important?

Tenochtitlán was the capital city of the Aztec **Empire**. It was built on an island in Lake Texcoco. The island had rich soil, and the nearby forests were good for gathering firewood and timber. Mountain rivers and streams emptied into the lake.

Water everywhere

Three giant raised roads called **causeways** joined the island to the mainland. People could easily walk back and forth. These amazing causeways were about 8 kilometres (5 miles) long and 7 metres (22 feet) wide.

This painting shows what Tenochtitlán, the island capital of the empire, would have looked like from above.

Tenochtitlán had both streets and canals. People often used canoes to get about on the canals. There were also lots of wide bridges that allowed people to cross the canals on foot.

The sacred district

In Tenochtitlán, like in every Aztec city, the **sacred** district was kept apart with high walls. Inside, there were many **pyramids** and **shrines**. The pyramids were called step-pyramids, because they had two sets of stairs, each of which led to a small shrine at the top. The Great Temple, which was the largest step-pyramid, was about 60 metres (200 feet) tall.

Homes

Nobles lived in the city centre. They owned stone palaces, which not only had a main house, but also bath houses, guest rooms, swimming pools, gardens, and courtyards. Some even had zoos!

Commoners lived outside the city centre in houses made of mud bricks called **adobe**. The roofs were made of straw. Neighbours would share an open courtyard, where people could meet and work together.

Heavy traffic

Lake Texcoco was very busy! At times, there were between 50,000 and 200,000 canoes on it, carrying people and goods to market.

Chinampas

The Aztecs invented a clever new way of farming. They built hundreds of raised fields called **chinampas** in the swamps around Tenochtitlán. These fields rested on beds of woven reeds. Farmers planted willow trees around the edges of the fields to hold the land in place. They scooped up mud from the bottom of the lake and piled it on to the chinampas to help their crops grow. Aztec farmers planted corn, tomatoes, beans, fruits, and flowers.

Here you can see what the Aztec chinampas would have looked like. They have been built in rows and planted with corn.

THEN...

Farmers dug mud from the bottom of the lakes to spread on their crops as fertilizer to help the plants grow. This mud included human waste that had been dumped into the canals. When the Spanish arrived, they noted that even though human waste ended up in the lake, the water did not smell bad like the rivers in Europe did. The Aztecs used the lake water for drinking, cooking, and washing.

Today, Mexico City's chinampas are a popular tourist attraction. Many people like to go on boat trips around the islands.

Island gardens

Chinampas still exist in Mexico City. They are no longer used for crops, but have become pretty island gardens that people like to visit.

...NOW

In the 1980s, scientists began studying Mexico City's chinampas. Human waste still drains into the canal waters. Even so, people who drink the water remain healthy. On further study, the scientists discovered a new kind of **bacteria** that quickly cleans the waste and makes it safe to use as fertilizer. Now some companies have begun putting the chinampas bacteria to work in areas without **sewer** systems. They add the helpful chinampas bacteria to compost toilet systems to destroy disease-causing bacteria.

How were the Aztecs conquered?

The Spanish **conquistadors**, led by Hernán Cortés, landed on the coast of Mexico in March 1519. They travelled inland, fighting, killing, and **conquering** the people they met along the way. Some of these people joined the invaders.

The Spanish reached Tenochtitlán in November. They took the *tlatoani*, Moctezuma II, hostage. For a while, Cortés ruled the city with Moctezuma's help.

This painting shows an artist's idea of what it would have been like when Moctezuma (right) was held hostage by Hernán Cortés and the conquistadors. How do you think Moctezuma would have felt?

City in ruins

In 1520, Moctezuma died. The new *tlatoani* led his warriors against the Spanish. The war lasted for months, ending in a Spanish victory in 1521. The Spanish killed priests and nobles, stole the city's gold, and destroyed its buildings.

The Aztecs were known for their skill as warriors. They were feared and respected by their neighbours. How were the Spanish able to defeat them? The Spanish had horses, cannons, and guns, while the Aztecs had spears and saw-swords. The Spanish fought to kill, while the Aztecs fought to take prisoners whom they would later give to the gods as **human sacrifices**. The Aztecs lost because the Spanish fought in ways they had never seen before.

The conquistadors built Mexico City where Tenochtitlán had stood. Over time, Spanish became the language of Mexico, and Christianity became its religion.

Aztec gifts

The Aztecs have done a lot for us today. Some Mexicans still speak **Nahuatl**, and some Nahuatl words have become part of the English language.
The Aztecs gave us tortillas, tamales, and chocolate. **Chinampas bacteria** are helping to keep people healthy. Scientists try to rediscover Aztec cures and treatments by studying their plants and medicines. Perhaps, one day, Aztec medicine will save your life!

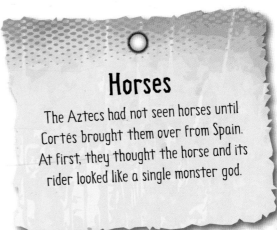

Horses

The Aztecs had not seen horses until Cortés brought them over from Spain. At first, they thought the horse and its rider looked like a single monster god.

Key dates

Here is an outline of important moments in the history and culture of the Aztec **Empire**:

around 1150   The Aztecs leave their home in Aztlan. The exact location of Aztlan is unknown.

1150–1200s   The Aztecs reach central Mexico

1325   Tenochtitlán is built on an island in Lake Texcoco

1325–1428   Workers construct a canal system in Tenochtitlán; Tenochtitlán grows in size and wealth

1390   Construction begins on a new **pyramid** in Tenochtitlán

1440   Moctezuma I begins a 29-year reign

1450–1454   Severe drought destroys the harvest and leaves thousands of people dead

1473   Aztecs **conquer** Tlateloco, a neighbouring island

1487   The Great Temple is rebuilt in Tenochtitlán

1502	Moctezuma II begins his reign
1519	Hernán Cortés arrives on the coast of Mexico in March; he reaches Tenochtitlán in November and enters the city as a guest of Moctezuma
1520	Cortés begins his assault on the Aztec Empire; Moctezuma dies; the next emperor, Cuitláhuac, drives the Spanish out of the city
1521	The Spanish and the Tlaxcalans attack Tenochtitlán and defeat the Aztecs; the last emperor, Cuauhtemoc, surrenders to Cortés on 13 August
1522	The Spanish build Mexico City on the ruins of Tenochtitlán

Glossary

adobe sun-dried mud bricks used as building material. Aztec farmers made their homes of adobe.

bacteria one-celled organism. Some bacteria are harmful to humans; others are helpful.

cacao bean bean from an evergreen tree used to produce chocolate. The Aztecs used cacao beans as money.

carmine red colour from cochineal insects. Carmine is used as a food colouring.

causeway raised road across wet or swampy areas. Tenochtitlán had three giant causeways.

chinampa man-made island garden used to produce food in swampy areas. Aztec farmers invented the chinampa.

cochineal insect insect that feeds off the prickly pear cactus and is used to make red dye

conquer take control of a city or a people by force. The Spanish conquered the Aztecs.

conquistador leader or soldier from Spain, who came to conquer Central and South America. Hernán Cortés was a conquistador.

diabetes illness in which the body cannot process sugar correctly

empire large territory governed by a powerful ruler. The Aztec Empire lasted for 94 years.

human sacrifice making an offering to the gods by killing a person. Human sacrifices were thought to bring good harvests.

Nahuatl language of the Aztecs. Nahuatl is still spoken by some Aztecs.

pyramid building with a square base that rises to a point. Aztec pyramids had two sets of stairs.

sacred used for religious purposes. Aztec pyramids were sacred.

sewers underground system for carrying away water with human toilet waste in it

shrine holy place. Aztecs built shrines on the top of their pyramids.

tlatoani Aztec word for emperor. Moctezuma II was a tlatoani.

tribute tax paid by people to the emperor. Commoners and defeated cities paid tributes.

Find out more

Books

All About Ancient Peoples: Aztecs and Incas, Anita Ganeri
(Franklin Watts, 2009)

Digging into History: Solving the Mysteries of Aztec Cities,
Anita Croy (Franklin Watts, 2010)

Uncovering the Past: The Aztecs, John Malam
(Evans Brothers, 2009)

Websites

aztecs.mrdonn.org
This website has lots of information on the history and
everyday life of the Aztecs.

www.azteccalendar.com/azteccalendar.html
Learn more about the Aztec calendar at this useful web page.

www.fieldmuseum.org/Chocolate/history.html
Visit this website to discover more about the history
of chocolate.

www.latinamericanstudies.org/aztecs.htm
This website contains lots of pictures of important Aztec sites,
objects, and artwork.

Index

माँ ने जिल से पूछा, "क्या है तुम्हारे पास उपाय
जिससे पैसा पा सकते हम बेच कर अपनी गाय?"

Mum asked Jill, "Do you think somehow
You could raise money selling our cow?"

जिल एक मील ही चली होगी उसे द्वार के पास एक आदमी मिला।

"गाय के बदले तुम यह बीन्स लो," उसने कहा।

"बीन्स!" जिल चिल्लाई "क्या तुम्हारा दिमाग खराब है?"

आदमी ने समझाया, "ये जादुई बीन्स है, ये तुम्हारे लिए उपहार लायेंगी जो तुमने देखा न होगा।"

Jill had barely walked a mile when she met a man beside a stile.

"Swap you these beans for that cow," he said.

"Beans!" cried Jill. "Are you off your head?"

The man explained, "These are magic beans. They bring you gifts you've never seen."

जिल उन्हें लेकर माँ को दिखाने घर चल पड़ी,
वह जोर से चिल्लाई, "मुझे बेटे को भेजना चाहिए था!"
उसने बीन्स को जिल के पैर पर दे मारा
और उसे भेज दिया सोने को कुछ खाए बिना।

Jill took them home to show her mum
Who cried out loud, "I should have sent my son!"
She threw the beans down at Jill's feet
And sent her to bed with nothing to eat.

जल्दी सोनेवाले, जल्दी जागे,
जिल भोर में एक बड़े आश्चर्य से उठी।
आकाश तक उग गया था एक बीनस्टॉक।
डंठल थामे, पत्तियों को जोर से पकड़ कर,
हवा से हिलते उस बड़े पौधे पर वह चढ़ गई।

Early to bed, early to rise,
Jill woke up at dawn with a mighty surprise.
A beanstalk had grown right up to the skies.
Catching hold of the stalk, clinging fast to the leaves,
She climbed the great plant as it swayed in the breeze.

जिल ने अपनी माँ की चिल्लाहट सुनी!
"तुरन्त नीचे आओ, अपने भाई की देखभाल करो!"
पर जिल चढ़ती ही गई, वह रुकी नहीं,
लगातार ऊपर की ओर, एक दम ऊपर तक।

Jill heard a shout, it was her mother!
"Come down at once, look after your brother!"
But Jill just kept on climbing, she didn't stop,
All the way upwards, right to the top.

वह बीन्सटॉक से कूद पड़ी, और सुना एक तेज रोना।
एक छोटी लड़की रोई, "ओह! कहाँ मेरी भेड़ गयीं?
वे कहीं चली गयीं जब मैं सो रही थी।"
"मैं कहाँ हूँ?" जिल ने पूछा।

She leapt off the beanstalk, and heard a loud weep.
A little girl cried, "Oh, where are my sheep?
They've wandered away while I was asleep."
"Where am I?" asked Jill.

"तुम वहाँ हो जहाँ दानव रहता है।
तुम आयी हो उससे बदला लेने या क्षमा करने?
मेरी छड़ी हिलाकर अब अपना भाग्य चुनो,
बीन्सटॉक के नीचे आने का या दानव के घर के द्वार जाने का?"

"You're in the land where the Giant lives.
Did you come to avenge or come to forgive?
With a wave of my crook now choose your fate,
Back down the beanstalk or onto the Giant's Gate?"

जिल दानव के घर के बाहर खड़ी थी
लगती छोटी और डरे चूहे की तरह दुबकी थी।
एक अन्जान बुढ़िया वहाँ खड़ी थी,
आसमान से जाले हटा रही थी।
"छोटी लड़की, तुम यहाँ क्यों आई हो? क्यों, ओह क्यों?"

Jill stood in front of the Giant's house
Feeling tiny and scared like a quivering mouse.
A strange old woman was standing by,
Brushing cobwebs out of the sky.
"Little girl, why are you here? Why, oh why?"

जैसे वह बोली धरती हिलने लगी, जोर से आवाज हुई लगा जैसे आया भूकंप।
बुढ़िया ने कहा, "जल्दी, भागो अन्दर! केवल छुप सकती होकृ. भट्टी के अन्दर!
धीरे से साँस लेना, न लेना आहें, बर्फ सी शान्त रहना, अगर नहीं चाहती मरना।"

As she spoke the ground began to shake, with a deafening sound like a mighty earthquake.
The woman said, "Quick run inside. There's only one place…in the oven you'll hide!
Take barely one breath, don't utter a sigh, stay silent as snow, if you don't want to die."

जिल दुबकी थी भट्टी में। यह उसने क्या कर डाला? उसने सोचा काश वह घर पर माँ के पास होती।
दानव बोला, "फी, फाइ, फा, फम। मुझे पश्थ्वी के आदमी के खून की आ रही है गंध।"
"पति, तुम्हे गंध आती है मेरे पकाइ चिड़ियों की पाई की। सभी चार और बीस जो आसमान से गिर पड़ी।"

Jill crouched in the oven. What had she done? How she wished she were home with her mum.
The Giant spoke, "Fee, fi, faw, fum. I smell the blood of an earthly man."
"Husband, you smell only the birds I baked in a pie. All four and twenty dropped out of the sky."

दानव गुर्राया, "मुझे तुम्हारे नाजुक व्यंजन चखने की भी नहीं इच्छा पत्नी, मुझे खाना चाहिए। रसोई में जाओ और मांस ले आओ!"
जिल ने भट्टी के दरवाजे के दरार से देखा, दानव ने बनैले सूअर को खा डाला।

The Giant bawled, "I have no wish to even try your dainty dish.
Wife, I need to eat. Go to the kitchen and fetch me my meat!"
From a gap in the oven door, Jill watched the Giant devour a wild boar.

दानव बैठ गया, पर खुश न था।
वह गरजा, "मुझे मेरी बतख दो,
और जल्दी से लाओ।"
कहते हुये "बतख अन्डा दो,"
उसने अपनी ऑंखें बन्द कर लिया।
जिल आश्चर्यचकित थी,
बतख ने एक चमकता सुनहरा अन्डा दिया।
दानव ने खूब मजे लिये,
एक से एक ठोस सोने के अन्डे गिने।
फिर वह सो गया और खर्राटा लेने लगा
लग रहा था जैसे शेर दहाड़ने लगा!

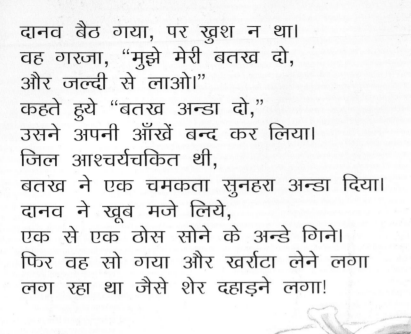

The Giant sat back, he wasn't happy.
He bellowed: "Get me my goose,
and make it snappy."
Saying: "Goose deliver," he closed his eyes.
It lay a bright golden egg,
much to Jill's surprise.
The Giant had a lot of fun,
Counting solid gold eggs one by one.
Then he fell asleep and started to snore
Sounding just like a mighty lion's roar!

जिल को था मालूम भाग सकती है वह दानव के सोते।
सावधानी से वह भट्टी के बाहर आयी।
उसे याद आया उसके मित्र टाम ने क्या किया था।
सूअर चुराकर भाग गया था।
बतख पकड़ कर वह भागी और भागी।
"मुझे बीन्सटॉक तक जल्द से जल्द पहुँचना होगा।"

Jill knew she could escape while the Giant slept.
So carefully out of the oven she crept.
Then she remembered what her friend, Tom, had done.
Stole a pig and away he'd run.
Grabbing the goose, she ran and ran.
"I must get to that beanstalk as fast as I can."

"मैं वापस आ गयी!", चिल्लाते वह डंठल से सरकी।
यह सुन जैक और माँ घर से बाहर निकली।

She slid down the stalk shouting, "I'm back!"
And out of the house came mother and Jack.

"मैं और तुम्हारा भाई, थे बहुत परेशान। कैसे उस बड़े डंठल पर चढ़ तुम गई आसमान?"
"पर माँ," जिल बोली, "मुझे कुछ नहीं हुआ। और देखो मेरे हाथ के नीचे क्या है।"
"बतख़ अन्डा दो," जिल ने दानव के बोले शब्द दोहराया,
और बतख़ ने तुरन्त एक चमकता सुनहरा अन्डा दिया।

"We've been worried sick, your brother and I. How could you climb that great stalk to the sky?"
"But mum," Jill said, "I came to no harm. And look what I have under my arm."
"Goose deliver," Jill repeated the words that the Giant had said,
And the goose instantly laid a bright golden egg.

जिल के दानव के घर जाने से उसके परिवार की भूख और निराशा मिट गई।

Jill's visit to the Giant's lair kept her family from hunger and despair.

जैक को अपने बहन से जलन होने लगी।
काश उसने पहाड़ी के बजाय बीन्सटॉक पर चढ़ाई की होती।
जैक डींग मारता और हरदम कहता।
यदि वह दानव से मिलता तो उसका सिर काट लिए होता।

Jack couldn't help feeling envious of his sister Jill.
He wished he'd climbed a beanstalk instead of a hill.
Jack boasted a lot and often said
If he'd met the Giant he would've chopped off his head.

उस डंठल पर चढ़ने से उनकी माँ ने मना कर रखा था।
पर जैक की खोखली बातों से जिल उब गयी थी।
एक दिन, जिल भेष बदल के, बीन्सटॉक पर चढ़ी
और आकाश में पहुँच गयी।

Their mother had warned them not to climb that stalk
But Jill was fed up with Jack's idle talk.
One day, in clever disguise, Jill climbed up the beanstalk
And reached the skies.

द्वार के पास बुढ़िया बैठी थी उदास,
बदमाश दानव ने उसके साथ बहुत बुरा बर्ताव किया
जब से उसकी बतख चोरी चली गयी थी,
हर दिन वह डरावना होता जा रहा था।

The old woman sat by the gate looking sad,
The evil Giant treated her bad, very bad.
He'd become more gruesome by the day,
Since his goose had been stolen away.

दानव की पत्नी जिल को पहचान न पायी,
पर उसने पहाड़ी से उतरती गरजते पैरों की आवाज सुनी।
वह चिल्लायी, "दानव! यदि अभी वह तुम्हारे खून को सूंघ लेगा, तो अवश्य मार डालेगा।"

The Giant's wife didn't recognise Jill,
But she heard the sound of thundering footsteps coming down the hill.
"The Giant!" she cried. "If he smells your blood now, he's sure to kill."

"हिकरी डिकरी डाक! जल्दी,
दिवार घड़ी के अन्दर छुप जाओ!"

"Hickory dickory dock,
quick, go hide in the clock!"

"फी, फाइ, फा, फम, मुझे पृथ्वी के आदमी के खून की आती है गंध।"
दानव ने कहा, "चाहे वह जिन्दा हो या मुर्दा, मैं उसकी गर्दन उड़ा दूँगा।"
"तुम्हे सिर्फ मेरे बनाए ताजे टार्टस की गंध मिली है, जो नुसखा मैंने दिल की रानी से ली है।"
"मैं दानव हूँ, पत्नी, मुझे खाना चाहिए। रसोई में जाओ और मेरा मांस ले आओ।"

"Fe fi faw fum, I smell the blood of an earthly man.
Let him be alive or let him be dead, I'll chop off his head," the Giant said.
"You smell only my freshly baked tarts, I borrowed a recipe from the Queen of Hearts."
"I'm a Giant, wife, I need to eat. Go to the kitchen and get me my meat."

पहले की तरह दानव ने जानवर को खा डाला।
एक घण्टे बाद, उसने और माँग कर डाला।
उसकी पत्नी हार्प ले आयी, जो था बहुत सुन्दर,
असली सोने से बना जिसमें लगे थे सौ तार अन्दर।
दानव चिल्लाया,"बजाओ!" उसे ऊब हो रही थी।
हार्प अपने आप बज उठा।

The Giant gorged on beast as before.
One full hour passed by, then he called for more.
His wife brought in a harp, the most magnificent of things,
Made out of pure gold with a hundred strings.
The Giant yelled: "Play," he was feeling bored.
The harp instantly played of its own accord.

शांत और मीठी धुन सुन दानव को जोर की नींद आ गयी।
जिल को अपने आप बजने वाला हार्प चाहिए था, उसे वह जरूर चाहिए था!
दिवार घड़ी से वह आशंकित सी निकली और स्वर्ण हार्प पकड़ लिया जबकी दानव सोता रहा।

A lullaby so calm and sweet, the lumbering Giant fell fast asleep.
Jill wanted the harp that played without touch. She wanted it so very much!
Out of the clock she nervously crept, and grabbed the harp of gold whilst the Giant slept.

जिल बीन्सटॉक से थी बंधी गोलाकार में भागते कुत्ते से टकरा पड़ी।
हार्प चिल्ला पड़ा,"मालिक! मालिक!" दानव जागा, ऊठा और उसके पीछे भागा।
जिल को मालूम था उसे तेज से तेज भागना होगा।

To the beanstalk Jill was bound, tripping over a dog, running round and round.
When the harp cried out: "MASTER! MASTER!" The Giant awoke, got up and ran after.
Jill knew she would have to run faster and faster.

दानव गुर्राया,"तुम सोचती हो भाग सकती हो!
पाईपर के बेटे टाम का क्या हुआ, देखो!"
हार्प पकड़ कर, जिल भागी और भागी,
"जितना जल्दी से जल्दी हो सके मुझे बीन्सटॉक तक पहुँचना होगा।"

The Giant howled, "So you think you can run!
Look what happened to Tom, the piper's son!"
Holding onto the harp, Jill ran and ran,
"I must get to that beanstalk as fast as I can."

वह डंठल से फिसली, हार्प चिल्लायाः "मालिक!"
वह भद्दा दानव गड़गड़ाते हुए पीछे आया।
जिल ने लकड़ी काटने की कुल्हाड़ी पकड़ी
और बीन्सटॉक को काट डाला जल्दी से जल्दी।

She slid down the stalk, the harp cried: "MASTER!"
The great ugly Giant came thundering after.
Jill grabbed the axe for cutting wood
And hacked down the beanstalk as fast as she could.

दानव के हर पग से डंठल हिलने लगा। जिल के कुल्हाड़ी मारने से दानव गिरने लगा।
नीचे और नीचे दानव तेजी से गिरा!
जैक, जिल और माँ आश्चर्य से देखते रहे जैसे जैसे दानव दस फीट नीचे गिरा।

Each Giant's step caused the stalk to rumble. Jill's hack of the axe caused the Giant to tumble.
Down down the Giant plunged!
Jack, Jill and mum watched in wonder, as the giant CRASHED, ten feet under.

जैक, जिल और उसकी माँ अब अपने दिन बिताते हैं,
सोने के हार्प पर गाने और कविताएं गाते हैं।

Jack, Jill and their mother now spend their days,
Singing songs and rhymes that the golden harp plays.

British Library Cataloguing-in-Publication Data:
a catalogue record for this book is available
from the British Library.

First published 2004 by Mantra
5 Alexandra Grove, London N12 8NU, UK
www.mantralingua.com